MW00737675

blue

eve gowan

WITHIN:

blue

PRELUDE

There's blue

There's green

Then there's everything in-between

Who are we to decide where one or the other begin?

To me what I call green or blue

May be different to you

That's fine

Maybe my world is a little bluer

Or was for a long time

Maybe when others saw a green glowing light

How I felt inside was duller

The undertone of my hues hidden by something
stronger

Maybe we need elements of blue to become new again

Either way this book is a little blue

But kind of green too

There's a thin line between colours

And how they may intertwine

Each perception of colour unique and complete

I knew a girl who saw a new hue with every word we
spoke

Every mood or thought

Who are we to change her mind?

Art is what we make of it

So I made a book called blue

And I hope it moves you like the ocean tides I floated in.

blue

SECTION ONE
deep

The Storm

You know how you can smell the rain coming
after a perfectly warm day?
Before the clouds even brush past the sun
You can feel
The air begin to change.
Especially when it's been one of those hot days
Part of you is almost excited to watch the weather
change.
Relieved even
To let your body cool off and relax.

Sometimes I look back on days like that.
Days that were perfect until the rain came.
Warm,
Summery,
Happy and bright.
Followed by this period of doubt where you can feel,
You can smell the changes building up.

Even when you know it's coming,
The rain always seems to start a few seconds before
you expected it.
Before you really needed it...
Each icy drop cuts through the previously warm air
Like a hot knife through butter.
The sizzle and splatter on the ground outside escalates

eve gowan

And you watch dry dirt
Become darker and fade away.
You know you must go inside then.
Before it gets too cold.

But sometimes you don't.
Sometimes you stand in that rain
And look up at the sky.
You close your eyes
Feel the droplets slowly decorate your face.
It's a feeling of refreshment
But still so surreal...
You remember not long ago
How beautiful the day was
And how warm you used to be.
You remain warm for now
But you feel it fading too
Like the colours in the sky.

Sometimes on days like these
The light grey clouds become deep dark monsters
And spit out more than rain.
They yell
Scream,
Flash and flood.
In times like those you find shelter
To escape the storm...

blue

I remember all those sunny memories with you.
The days I thought were so perfect they could never
end.
The light,
The fresh air,
The heat on my skin.
I would bask in that sunlight.
I see now,
When that sun began to fade.
Although it will always remain
In the sky above us;
The clouds have covered up those days like a blanket.

For a while I have let the droplets run down my face.
Standing in our storm.
Closing my eyes,
Holding on to the last few fragments of our warmth and
sunshine.
But the rain is too heavy now,
It doesn't matter how hard I clutch
To the memories of how this day used to be
This storm is inevitable.
I'm getting colder
And the mere memory of warmth is no longer enough.

So all I can do is close the door,

Dry myself off,
And wait patiently for a better day.
A whole new day.
Where I can stand in this rain
Without memories to keep me warm.
On this day
I will be prepared for any change in weather.
I will be stronger,
Capable, independent.
I will be positive, adventurous,
Everything I need to be.
I won't have to go inside
Because the storm won't be us.
The storm won't be you giving up on me.
The storm will be whatever life throws at me
And this time,
I will have the choice to stand there and fight.

blue

Pins and needles
in my head
I forget,
how it felt
to be warmed
by you.

Metal boot
on my chest,
I lose the feeling
of loving you.

Breath caught
in my throat,
I may never
trust again.

My body
is drifting,
because you broke my heart.

Broken

Yet on the outside I feel myself smile
More and more each day
My body still functioning
The way it always has
Carrying me through every hour faithfully.
I'm still broken
How do I know?
Because something is missing from me
What that is exactly
Just seems to slip away
Like a sweet dream you once had
Yet can't remember.

blue

I saw the best in us
while you looked for ways
you needed to be without me.

eve gowan

I know a heart can't physically break
but I have learned the squeezing
suffocating
pain
that radiates from the center of my chest
how can something so *emotional*
become such *physical* torture?

blue

You hurt me.
Like the burning heat of the sun
nothing stops the pain
Like the wind
So strong
I can barely breathe.

You hurt me like the sunset beauty
Quickly replaced
With a sky of darkness.
You hurt me like the rain
Prickles of cold water numbing my skin.

You hurt me to my bones.
Every cell in my body
Aches
From what you have done
And fumes
At the thought
That you were powerful enough to do it.

eve gowan

I saw a future and
you saw a dream that won't come true
I saw love...
You saw you.

blue

in my dreams my heart searches for an answer,
waking up with more questions than before
feeling the ghosts
of exes on my shoulders,
reminders of what nightmares faced me in slumber
feelings so vivid
yet images blurred,
it's like they were with me
but
never were.

Broken Pieces

Heartbreak aftermath.
Shards of my fragile love splayed around me.
Every time I went to collect the next piece
Something else would nudge me out of balance,
Make me drop everything I had
And watch it shatter all over again.

Since then, I've been getting better
At picking up bits of me that were broken
But sometimes I can't quite figure out
Where they need to go.
I think I've lost a few too.
Scars growing over the empty spaces.
I look at them now
And remember how easy things used to be...

One thing after the other,
Losing so much so fast,
Left me beaten down.
Learning how dark the world can get
Destroying flashlights.
I stumble in darkness,
Cutting my feet and toes
On the parts I forgot to pick up months ago.
I guess you could say I'm both lost and broken too.

But
I don't want to wait for someone to fix me.
I don't want to feel them trace my scars with their
fingertips
So softly
And tell me I'm going to be okay.
I don't want to find a person who can hold me so
sincerely
That I collapse in their embrace.
I don't want to fall for that person because they remind
me
Of good feelings.
The ones I forgot how to feel
While I was caught up in my traumas.
I don't want to be in love
And feel at home in their body heat,
With that affection I so deeply crave.
I don't want to want that.
I don't want to long for the feeling of them
Wiping my tears away
Calling me strong,
And showing me all the new ways I can look at life
Because life hurts
They'd probably just break my heart all over again.

eve gowan

how is it
that you can
only measure
the love
you had for them
in metrics
of the pain
you feel
once they are lost?

Galaxy Love.

is what I called our playlist.
full of songs I thought
described the beginning of our journey

naive of me to believe that we were star crossed lovers
when our signs would never align.
elements of us so polar opposite
no wonder I couldn't start a fire in you,
when you were so deep underwater.

looking to space where planets revolve
in romantic galactic dance moves.
thinking we could be like them.

as the stars fill the sky above us
I wonder what it's like
to be so far away from a planet.
but now I know...
we weren't destined
we didn't fit.

we used to share our secrets under the moonlight
but now you're galaxies away from me.

I'm floating out here in this cold place,
because you changed the rules of gravity.

you changed, your mind.
now I have a playlist
of empty songs
describing a love,
that vanished like a falling star
I never even got to wish upon.

blue

I think of you when I brush my teeth
when I see the sky
and the moon too,
I think of you.
when people ask me how I am
I might lie when I say I'm fine.
but I think of you when their lips are on mine.
I'm fine as I brush my teeth alone,
shower on my own,
sleep in my own company...
sometimes.
when I don't
it's because I'm broken really
then I think of you
and all the others
who saw an angel
yet merely used her wings to fly.

Did you notice I could have drowned trying to fix you?
When all you had to do was come up for air...

blue

last night
I was swimming in the memories of you
rolling in dreams
tossing and turning in all your voices
drowning
in what could have been.

last night
you never left my mind alone
a fragment of what used to be
years later.

I feel as if I spent the night with you
yet I slept alone
and woke up guilty
because sometimes
somehow
I miss you.

eve gowan

I hoped and prayed and fell for your spell.
You talked and played and drew me in.

But you didn't want me,
You never did.

blue

my sad eyes look the same to you
on the outside they may appear
just as green and thoughtful as they always were
if you look close enough
you may notice slight changes
a little glassier,
a little smaller.

my sad eyes see you differently now
longing,
searching,
for what is no longer in sight
a little darker,
a little blurrier.

my sad eyes don't smile the same
it's easier to frown now
these eyes
used to be overflowing
with love and passion for you,
now all they seem to do
is leak
like a dripping tap no one could be bothered fixing.

Silly of me to compare our love to the entire universe
when it was over in the blink of an eye

blue

two weeks

or less

it took you to be over me.

two weeks

or more

it took me to realize I never really caught your eye.

eight months

I guess

of building something from a fantasy.

one night

or four

where you broke my trust and made me cry.

Touch sensitive.
cold,
& numb
scared
to be warmed by another.

Anxious.
pins,
& needles
disseminate
from skin
to bone.

blue

I thought this new heartbreak would be easier
because I've done it all before
being left behind
let down
betrayed
but I still want you to play me your songs as I fall asleep
every night
I still want to hear your art
I want to lay before you
and fall for you
while you fall for your guitar
I want you to stroke my face again
lie to me
tell me I am all you truly need
I want you to lie one more time for me
I want you to think about how maybe I could be right for
you
change your dreams
and put me in them
realise you don't want to chase the lust cloud down a
rainy path
follow me,
the sunshine.
I thought this heartbreak would be easier
but you were never truly mine.

Please don't fall in love with me.
I'm still broken from the last time,
And I can't do it all again
I'm not ready
To give a heart to someone
When I'm still piecing mine back together
So
Please don't fall in love with me
I could not possibly
Give you what you need
When I never got it myself

You're looking at cracked stain glass
Where the art seems better from afar
Yet up close
Even a touch could break me
And a kiss rip me in half
You don't deserve just half of me
Maybe
When I'm whole
I'll let you fall in love with me
Of course
Only then will you be gone.

blue

SECTION TWO
dark

I really want to write about it...
my feelings
my journey
my lessons
I want to write about my experiences
and my downfalls

I want to be able to describe them
the way beautiful authors do
in their enchanting phrases
make you feel things you didn't even know were real
I want to do that
I want to explain how hard it has been lately
how much pain I have felt, how lonely I have been
but it's as if
my words are blurred and misconstrued
like bubbles under water

I want to explain to everyone who
has doubted and left me
that I'm so sick of being quiet
to say how fucking angry I am
that bad things happen to good people
while bad people walk away free

but people who
put the world above their own needs

and live like glowing selfless angels
are stomped on by the dark feet of demons
who only ever look down.

I want to sit here and ask why people like me
get dealt shit like this
and hear back the words
'because you're stronger than them'
and maybe I am.

maybe those angels who serve to please others,
 spreading light and love,
will use those strong abilities
to remind those demons of their place
maybe my lesson
is to realise how lucky I was
to be given such a challenging life,
because every single day I grow in strength
while those tiny demonic people
are handed a boring life on a silver platter
that will teach them nothing but regret.

Burning anger.
Black smoke.
Cold heart.
Deadly eyes.
Warrior.

blue

You get so cold in the ocean,
but never hesitated to let the currents of your own
ambitions
pull you worlds away from me.

eve gowan

I remember you saying you've never met one as kind as
I
but that was before you gave me a reason
to remove my compassion
just as quickly as you broke your word.

blue

I have you in my tapestry,
nothing can erase...

but time unravels;
now I'm the one you can't replace.

Snake

(Eve)

I've shed my skin
Since the last time you touched me,
Though I watch you slither quickly away.
Tell me your heart is with me,
And let her take you home.

I've shed my skin
Since the last time you touched her,
So, you've lost the power
To tempt me with an apple.
For I know where just one bite will take me,
To the place where sins weave seamlessly,
With the stories
You tell yourself.

I've shed my skin
Since the last time you saw me
But yours is the bite that will poison us,
Not mine.
My fire has never burned this furiously
Fueled by your broken promises and deception.

What we had was far from wonderful
And nowhere close to real.
Because real would require honesty,

blue

And you never learnt
How to use that did you?
Your body built itself on lies
So that every time
You shed, your skin
You'd tangle yourself in fake realities
And get lost all over again.
Too deep to notice how many others
You dragged down with you.

Because you're destined to be alone
With everyone you'll ever know
Never giving them your everything
Like I gave you mine.

One day
In years to come
Maybe you will ask me
Where did I go wrong?
And I will tell you
Darling,
You're the only thing you've ever truly loved.

eve gowan

I scream loud when nobody can hear me
My roar shaking the walls to every corner of my mind
The fire inside me burning high
The anger keeping me alive.

-- *Lion.*

blue

You can't command me
You could barely control the ripples of your own
mistakes.

eve gowan

because I could never call you
I write all this to replace that
to replace all the yelling and crying
I would do on my end of the phone
yelling to you.

so here I am now
screaming my heart out on these pages
hoping you will hear my pain
or better yet
feel it for me.

blue

You can't look into my soul
and tell me I resemble a mystical being
if you don't believe in magic.

-

You can't pretend you know how to swim
if you don't know the difference
between the waves of your emotions
and the ones caused by everyone else in your waters.

eve gowan

he moved her in a way
a fresh candle wick
opens up to their first flame...
innocently oblivious,
to how well she is going to burn.

blue

Unsatisfied.
Is how I feel when I think about you
And what we had
Not broken.
Just devastatingly disappointed.

It's like digging something up
You know should stay buried.
Letting a past love,
Back into your heart.

blue

When the sun goes down
And the lion sleeps,
I become the maiden.
Serving others
With all that I have
Leaving nothing for myself.

-- *star signs.*

Yet I am still rising
You revolve around me
I am the sun
I rule the planets
And my fire is burning hotter than ever
Fueled by the amount of pain and disappointment
Those lost boys gifted me.

blue

.

SECTION THREE
aqua

eve gowan

Now I'm thinking of after the rain.
The settling.
The slowing.
How the sun gleams
Through the remaining raindrops
Like falling glitter.
The way everything
Just
Shines.

Before the drops warm
And rise back up into the sky.
How the flowers open
To soak up the water and sun together.

It's important
To see that life relies on the storm.
Trees need to fight the wind
In order to learn to dig their roots deeper
And stay standing.
We need the sun to go away sometimes.
We need to know darkness.
But not forever.
We need pain
To remember how good it feels to be without it.
Every life has its seasons.
Every day has its night.

My garden,
My forest
Has felt all kinds of winter,
Rain
And storm;
Now it's learning how to thaw out.
Warm, blossom, and bloom.
To grow taller than ever,
Roots intertwined,
Like my family's fingertips at every funeral.

all of that lost potential glistening in the night air
so bright
you feel your heart drop
when you see it

remembering how I wished to be the sky

now you see me every time you look up.

blue

I am way more valuable
than a moment of weakness,
or a drunken mistake.

eve gowan

Sometimes our memories catch us by surprise

In the breeze

In the sunshine

As we drive through old streets

And those memories

Will come alive

As we sleep.

blue

There is a certain beauty in pain
Hot tears trickle and shine
Like the purest form of water.

Pain challenges us
Changes us.

Emotion so powerful
Even the strongest go weak.

My heart is an eclipse.

The crescent moon shines a warmth in half my heart
while the other shines for you.

The full moon recharges the energy inside my soul.

blue

It's funny how our lives have chapters.
Every person
A book
Being read at their own pace.
Sometimes our chapters overlap
And lives are read in sync
For years and years.

It's funny how a few chapters ago
You were a mere stranger in my book.
After the words in our pages met
We fell into knowing one another back to front.
Folding the pages of our lives
To mark memories we wanted to hold on to.

But when we changed pace
One of us left the other behind
To start a new chapter.
Our intertwined pages being pulled apart.

I look at you now like that stranger again.
Knowing the pages we had together
Are behind us
And I need to keep reading alone.

But don't fret.
I won't burn or rip out the pages

Of the long chapter we once shared.

They are a part of me as much as they are you.

The ink a little smudged

But illustrations all the same

Of a love that was once brand new.

blue

I am a lion
But I'd never lie to you
Just when we lay together
I'll keep my claws concealed.

recently I've realized just how *fucking* messy life can
get.
just when you think you've seen it all,
life reminds you how ugly it can become.
my naive thoughts about this world have shattered
like the hearts of families forever broken.

broken glass pieces of this once beautiful mural
ask to be restructured
I am making a piece of art now
to remind me just how different life can be
to how it was once imagined
although I am shattered now
I won't give up on rebuilding my life.
I know there is more to come.

as broken glass can look so pretty.
microscopic cracks reflecting all kinds of light.
life is fragile and breakable,
it's about what you decide to do with that damage.

only then
can life
truly
become art.

blue

Memories come to life in our dreams
Our minds casting spells
Playing with magic
Powerful enough
To wake us up in tears, screaming
Gentle enough
To conjure a laugh or smile.

eve gowan

Earth angel
Blood flowing in my veins
Like river systems to the sea
My eyes leak salt water
I'm alive and I breathe what the trees give me
Though my branches don't reach the sun
Leaves fall from my fingertips
Like shedding skin
I'm as cold and bare as the winter.
I will wait for spring to come
To bring new beginnings
New life
Maybe then I will forgive my past
And let my roots meet
The deepest connections
Of the earth.

blue

SECTION FOUR
light

everyone holds the power to hurt me
but they may also change my life
I won't run from the pain any longer

blue

Loving someone
and being in love *with* them.
In sync
are two very different languages.

eve gowan

Our tears carry the memories
of what we once held so precious.

It's funny how the past makes you think
That the future is limited
To what has happened before
Who can or can't hurt us
But the truth is
The past is one second of reality
Gone in an instant
And the future is moments away
Diversified with beauty
Waiting to be seen with fresh eyes.

eve gowan

I want a love like rain
a touch that tingles
kisses that taste like the sky
dances in puddles
I want to be loved like rain
where every second is magic

blue

In smoke filled lungs
Blazing lights
Toxic company
Shallow nights
You don't find love there

Cigarette hangovers
Distractions,
sickness
Running from reality
Chasing temporary fixes
Love won't live there

Love lives in the present.
Empty forests
Blank pages
Open arms
Warm faces
Love waits for you there.
To stop
Listen
And worship your own soul.

eve gowan

beauty scars
angel color on your skin
the stretch
from where the goddess wakes within.

perfect imperfections
of your inner beauty
painted oh-so flawlessly.

wear them with pride
for your purity,
will never want to hide.

blue

Twilight nights
Clouds race
In moonlit height
Like puppeteers
Pulling strings of fate
Until we collide again.

Full moon magic
Bright like day at midnight
May we recharge our hearts
Like our crystals left in cars
As we walk through moonlit forests.

This is the moon dance
Simple at a glance,
But fate does not tread lightly
Magic is precise.

There's music in the sky you see
Wind fighting our reality,
It's like a dream
On a movie screen
That night
When the moon could set the scene.

We hold magic in the memories of our minds.

And now I look forward to heartbreaks
Not because of romance
Because of pain
From loving so many
But watching them leave.
Feeling them lie.
I look forward to the pain
Because it motivates creation
Passion in art.
Without their disappointments
I wouldn't have enough tragedies
to fill these pages

I'd run out of things to say.

-- Motivation

If you must know
It did not take meeting you
To know I was healing
Because *you* are just a version of me
I had been waiting for
But the truth is
I left the old version behind
A long time ago

blue

We're not in a race
but if we were
I've been giving you hurdles
and you succeeded
over every single one
with ease

you say I brought color back into your world
but you brought life back into mine
parts of me so dormant
cold
you helped light me up again
crawl out of my winter
and spring into your arms

blue

I don't know how to write about us
Because you are nothing like I've ever had before
You are new to me
Brand new

eve gowan

with a spark strong enough to light my fire
you bring the lion back to life
and nurse the maiden in me
with a heart & hands gentle as water

-- *horoscopes*

blue

You are the greatest work of art
My hands have ever touched
I could look into your galaxy eyes
For lifetimes.

I'm in love again
With who I am
So the people who enter my world now
Shall see it the way it's always wanted to be
And together we
Will grow
Like the forests I've planted long ago
And our love will flow
Like the rivers below
In my world
Built by me
Open to anyone who
Can see
That treating me the way I deserve
Is the only option
To receive my love

blue

SNEAK PEAK
green

I don't have much to say
but I want to talk about the wind
The power of the wind
In her hair
In the tree branches
Along the beach
It can be everywhere and nowhere in an instant
It can push, carry, pull and break
So strong and violent
Yet so easily will it calm my mind on a rainy night
So loud and cold
It can take my breath and run away with it
Take my voice
The voices of everyone it touches
And rush into nothingness
With the loudest silence there ever was

blue

close your eyes
let the rain
coat your skin
melt away the pain
every drop
cleansing

you show me love like springtime
as the flowers awake
blossoms bless the treescapes
you show me new beginnings
as the days grow
slowly warmer
the skies above us
paint wonder
we speak to the clouds
and you bring my heart home.

blue

Acknowledgements

I would like to formally thank each and every person
who assisted me in the process of sharing this book
with the world.
To those who inspired the feelings required for
conjuring these poems; thank you.
The pain was worth my growth.

About The Author
Eve Gowan

Eve is a young self-published author. She has been writing and sharing poetry since 2019, although Blue is her first published book. Eve plans on releasing more books in the future. She is a university graduate with a passion for sustainability and climate change solutions. If you would like to learn more about Eve, you can visit her website allwayseve.com and find her socials.

Printed in the USA
CPSIA information can be obtained
at www.ICGtesting.com
LVHW071924180823
755634LV00012BA/195